# Domenico Scarlatti

# GREAT KEYBOARD SONATAS

## Series II

Dover Publications, Inc.
New York

Published in Canada by General Publishing Company, Ltd., 30 Lesmill Road, Don Mills, Toronto, Ontario.
Published in the United Kingdom by Constable and Company, Ltd.

This Dover edition, first published in 1986, is a new selection of sonatas from D. *Scarlatti, Opere complete per clavicembalo*, edited by Alessandro Longo, as published in eleven volumes, 1906–08, by G. Ricordi & C., Milan. The table of contents, concordance, and Publisher's Note have been prepared specially for the present edition; see the Publisher's Note for further bibliographical information.

Manufactured in the United States of America
Dover Publications, Inc., 31 East 2nd Street, Mineola, N.Y. 11501

**Library of Congress Cataloging in Publication Data**

Scarlatti, Domenico, 1685–1757.
    [Sonatas, harpsichord. Selections]
    Great keyboard sonatas.

    v. of music.
    "This Dover edition, first published in 1986, is a new selection of sonatas from D. Scarlatti, Opere complete per clavicembalo, edited by Alessandro Longo, as published in eleven volumes, 1906–08, by G. Ricordi & C., Milan."
    1. Sonatas (Harpsichord)   I. Title.
M23.S28L65   1986                          85-752072
ISBN 0-486-24996-4 (ser. 1)
ISBN 0-486-25003-2 (ser. 2)

# PUBLISHER'S NOTE

This Dover edition of the later keyboard sonatas of Domenico Scarlatti reprints the musical texts from the edition prepared by Alessandro Longo in 1906–08. Scholarly research in more recent times has shed considerable light on keyboard practice in the Baroque era. It is obvious that the Longo edition, pioneering and monumental though it was, preceded such research and did not have its advantages. Longo conceived his edition for performance by the piano in place of the original instrument, the harpsichord. The edition thus includes traditional pianistic markings—the use of pedal, slurs, staccati, dynamics, including crescendi and diminuendi—as well as ornamentation now generally considered inappropriate; moreover, Longo's absolute indications of tempi were foreign to Scarlatti. The suggestions of phrasing and contrasting dynamics lie within the music itself rather than through explicit indication.

This is not to suggest that these sonatas can be played only on the harpsichord, but the performer on the piano should endeavor to approach the historical style as closely as possible. In the interest of providing an affordable edition, however, the pianistic elements of phrasing, dynamics, and pedal remain as they appear in the Longo edition. (The actual notation—pitches and lengths—is reliable and beautifully engraved.)

The performer desiring to understand more fully the interpretation of these sonatas is urged to consult the definitive study, *Domenico Scarlatti*, by the distinguished harpsichordist and scholar Ralph Kirkpatrick (Princeton University Press, 1953; paperback edition published by Thomas Y. Crowell, 1968), with particular attention to chapter 12, pages 280–323, on "The Performance of the Scarlatti Sonatas."

The numbers assigned to the sonatas in Kirkpatrick's study are used throughout the present edition. Following is a three-way concordance of the Kirkpatrick [K] numbers, the Pestelli [P] numbers (from Giorgio Pestelli, *Le sonate di Domenico Scarlatti: proposta di un ordinamento cronologico*, Turin, 1967), and the Longo [L] numbers (from Alessandro Longo, ed., *D. Scarlatti, Opere complete per clavicembalo*, Milan, 1906–08); only the sonatas included in the Dover edition are represented in this concordance.

At the end of each sonata will be found a statement, in full or in abbreviation—C.V., C.S., or E.O.—indicating Longo's source for the musical text. The Longo edition was based upon three sources: (1) One of the two complete fifteen-volume sets of manuscript copies made by a Spanish scribe. The copy Longo used—designated C.V. by him for Codice Veneziano—is at the Biblioteca Marciana, in Venice; the other copy is at the Arrigo Boito Conservatorio library, in Parma. (2) Italian copies in the Santini Collection—designated C.S. for Codice Santini—including five volumes now at Münster and seven volumes, once the property of Johannes Brahms, now at the Gesellschaft der Musikfreunde library, Vienna. (3) The edition of thirty sonatas published in London in 1738 under the title *Essercizi per gravicembalo*—designated E.O. for Edizione Originale.

| Kirkpatrick | Pestelli | Longo | Kirkpatrick | Pestelli | Longo | Kirkpatrick | Pestelli | Longo | Kirkpatrick | Pestelli | Longo |
|---|---|---|---|---|---|---|---|---|---|---|---|
| 478 | 503 | 12 | 498 | 367 | 350 | 518 | 390 | 116 | 538 | 542 | 254 |
| 479 | 380 | S16 | 499 | 477 | 193 | 519 | 445 | 475 | 539 | 543 | 121 |
| 480 | 381 | S8 | 500 | 358 | 492 | 520 | 362 | 86 | 540 | 544 | S17 |
| 481 | 504 | 187 | 501 | 385 | 137 | 521 | 429 | 408 | 541 | 545 | 120 |
| 482 | 356 | 435 | 502 | 408 | 3 | 522 | 526 | S25 | 542 | 546 | 167 |
| 483 | 407 | 472 | 503 | 196 | 196 | 523 | 527 | 490 | 543 | 547 | 227 |
| 484 | 428 | 419 | 504 | 265 | 29 | 524 | 528 | 283 | 544 | 548 | 497 |
| 485 | 490 | 153 | 505 | 386 | 326 | 525 | 529 | 188 | 545 | 549 | 500 |
| 486 | 515 | 455 | 506 | 409 | 70 | 526 | 530 | 456 | 546 | 550 | 312 |
| 487 | 421 | 205 | 507 | 478 | 113 | 527 | 531 | 458 | 547 | 551 | S28 |
| 488 | 382 | S37 | 508 | 516 | 19 | 528 | 532 | 200 | 548 | 552 | 404 |
| 489 | 522 | S41 | 509 | 387 | 311 | 529 | 533 | 327 | 549 | 553 | S1 |
| 490 | 476 | 206 | 510 | 525 | 277 | 530 | 534 | 44 | 550 | 554 | S42 |
| 491 | 484 | 164 | 511 | 388 | 314 | 531 | 535 | 430 | 551 | 555 | 396 |
| 492 | 443 | 14 | 512 | 359 | 339 | 532 | 536 | 223 | 552 | 556 | 421 |
| 493 | 383 | S24 | 513 | 176 | S3 | 533 | 537 | 395 | 553 | 557 | 425 |
| 494 | 444 | 287 | 514 | 389 | 1 | 534 | 538 | 11 | 554 | 558 | S21 |
| 495 | 384 | 426 | 515 | 417 | 255 | 535 | 539 | 262 | 555 | 559 | 477 |
| 496 | 332 | 372 | 516 | 523 | S12 | 536 | 540 | 236 | | | |
| 497 | 357 | 146 | 517 | 517 | 266 | 537 | 541 | 293 | | | |

| Longo | Kirkpatrick | Pestelli | Longo | Kirkpatrick | Pestelli | Longo | Kirkpatrick | Pestelli | Longo | Kirkpatrick | Pestelli |
|---|---|---|---|---|---|---|---|---|---|---|---|
| 1 | 514 | 389 | 188 | 525 | 529 | 326 | 505 | 386 | 477 | 555 | 559 |
| 3 | 502 | 408 | 193 | 499 | 477 | 327 | 529 | 533 | 490 | 523 | 527 |
| 11 | 534 | 538 | 196 | 503 | 196 | 339 | 512 | 359 | 492 | 500 | 358 |
| 12 | 478 | 503 | 200 | 528 | 532 | 350 | 498 | 367 | 497 | 544 | 548 |
| 14 | 492 | 443 | 205 | 487 | 421 | 372 | 496 | 332 | 500 | 545 | 549 |
| 19 | 508 | 516 | 206 | 490 | 476 | 395 | 533 | 537 | S1 | 549 | 553 |
| 29 | 504 | 265 | 223 | 532 | 536 | 396 | 551 | 555 | S3 | 513 | 176 |
| 44 | 530 | 534 | 227 | 543 | 547 | 404 | 548 | 552 | S8 | 480 | 381 |
| 70 | 506 | 409 | 236 | 536 | 540 | 408 | 521 | 429 | S12 | 516 | 523 |
| 86 | 520 | 362 | 254 | 538 | 542 | 419 | 484 | 428 | S16 | 479 | 380 |
| 113 | 507 | 478 | 255 | 515 | 417 | 421 | 552 | 556 | S17 | 540 | 544 |
| 116 | 518 | 390 | 262 | 535 | 539 | 425 | 553 | 557 | S21 | 554 | 558 |
| 120 | 541 | 545 | 266 | 517 | 517 | 426 | 495 | 384 | S24 | 493 | 383 |
| 121 | 539 | 543 | 277 | 510 | 525 | 430 | 531 | 535 | S25 | 522 | 526 |
| 137 | 501 | 385 | 283 | 524 | 528 | 435 | 482 | 356 | S28 | 547 | 551 |
| 146 | 497 | 357 | 287 | 494 | 444 | 455 | 486 | 515 | S37 | 488 | 382 |
| 153 | 485 | 490 | 293 | 537 | 541 | 456 | 526 | 530 | S41 | 489 | 522 |
| 164 | 491 | 484 | 311 | 509 | 387 | 458 | 527 | 531 | S42 | 550 | 554 |
| 167 | 542 | 546 | 312 | 546 | 550 | 472 | 483 | 407 | | | |
| 187 | 481 | 504 | 314 | 511 | 388 | 475 | 519 | 445 | | | |

| Pestelli | Kirkpatrick | Longo | Pestelli | Kirkpatrick | Longo | Pestelli | Kirkpatrick | Longo | Pestelli | Kirkpatrick | Longo |
|---|---|---|---|---|---|---|---|---|---|---|---|
| 176 | 513 | S3 | 390 | 518 | 116 | 517 | 517 | 266 | 542 | 538 | 254 |
| 196 | 503 | 196 | 407 | 483 | 472 | 522 | 489 | S41 | 543 | 539 | 121 |
| 265 | 504 | 29 | 408 | 502 | 3 | 523 | 516 | S12 | 544 | 540 | S17 |
| 332 | 496 | 372 | 409 | 506 | 70 | 525 | 510 | 277 | 545 | 541 | 120 |
| 356 | 482 | 435 | 417 | 515 | 255 | 526 | 522 | S25 | 546 | 542 | 167 |
| 357 | 497 | 146 | 421 | 487 | 205 | 527 | 523 | 490 | 547 | 543 | 227 |
| 358 | 500 | 492 | 428 | 484 | 419 | 528 | 524 | 283 | 548 | 544 | 497 |
| 359 | 512 | 339 | 429 | 521 | 408 | 529 | 525 | 188 | 549 | 545 | 500 |
| 362 | 520 | 86 | 443 | 492 | 14 | 530 | 526 | 456 | 550 | 546 | 312 |
| 367 | 498 | 350 | 444 | 494 | 287 | 531 | 527 | 458 | 551 | 547 | S28 |
| 380 | 479 | S16 | 445 | 519 | 475 | 532 | 528 | 200 | 552 | 548 | 404 |
| 381 | 480 | S8 | 476 | 490 | 206 | 533 | 529 | 327 | 553 | 549 | S1 |
| 382 | 488 | S37 | 477 | 449 | 193 | 534 | 530 | 44 | 554 | 550 | S42 |
| 383 | 493 | S24 | 478 | 507 | 113 | 535 | 531 | 430 | 555 | 551 | 396 |
| 384 | 495 | 426 | 484 | 491 | 164 | 536 | 532 | 223 | 556 | 552 | 421 |
| 385 | 501 | 137 | 490 | 485 | 153 | 537 | 533 | 395 | 557 | 553 | 425 |
| 386 | 505 | 326 | 503 | 478 | 12 | 538 | 534 | 11 | 558 | 554 | S21 |
| 387 | 509 | 311 | 504 | 481 | 187 | 539 | 535 | 262 | 559 | 555 | 477 |
| 388 | 511 | 314 | 515 | 486 | 455 | 540 | 536 | 236 | | | |
| 389 | 514 | 1 | 516 | 508 | 19 | 541 | 537 | 293 | | | |

# CONTENTS

| | | | |
|---|---|---|---|
| Sonata in D Minor, K516 | 1 | Sonata in A Major, K536 | 74 |
| Sonata in D Minor, K517 | 5 | Sonata in A Major, K537 | 78 |
| Sonata in F Major, K518 | 10 | Sonata in G Major, K538 | 82 |
| Sonata in F Minor, K519 | 14 | Sonata in G Major, K539 | 86 |
| Sonata in G Major, K520 | 18 | Sonata in F Major, K540 | 90 |
| Sonata in G Major, K521 | 22 | Sonata in F Major, K541 | 94 |
| Sonata in G Major, K522 | 26 | Sonata in F Major, K542 | 98 |
| Sonata in G Major, K523 | 30 | Sonata in F Major, K543 | 102 |
| Sonata in F Major, K524 | 33 | Sonata in B-flat Major, K544 | 106 |
| Sonata in F Major, K525 | 36 | Sonata in B-flat Major, K545 | 109 |
| Sonata in C Minor, K526 | 39 | Sonata in G Minor, K546 | 113 |
| Sonata in C Major, K527 | 43 | Sonata in G Major, K547 | 117 |
| Sonata in B-flat Major, K528 | 46 | Sonata in C Major, K548 | 122 |
| Sonata in B-flat Major, K529 | 49 | Sonata in C Major, K549 | 126 |
| Sonata in E Major, K530 | 52 | Sonata in B-flat Major, K550 | 131 |
| Sonata in E Major, K531 | 56 | Sonata in B-flat Major, K551 | 135 |
| Sonata in A Minor, K532 | 60 | Sonata in D Minor, K552 | 139 |
| Sonata in A Major, K533 | 64 | Sonata in D Minor, K553 | 143 |
| Sonata in D Major, K534 | 68 | Sonata in F Major, K554 | 147 |
| Sonata in D Major, K535 | 70 | Sonata in F Minor, K555 | 151 |

# Sonata in D Minor, K516

1

# Sonata in D Minor, K517

C.V. Libro XIII, N. 4. *(e)*

**27** (and similar) – C.V. *a)*

# Sonata in F Major, K518

C. V. Libro XIII N. 5. *(i)*

16 _ C. V. *a)*     22 _ C. V. *b)*

# Sonata in F Minor, K519

C. V. Libro XIII, N. 6. (e)

49 – (e simili)   (y similes)      a) Formula del trillo:   *Fórmula del trino:*
   *(et semblables)* (and similar)      *Formule du trille:*   Formula of the trill:

# Sonata in G Major, K520

C.V. Libro XIII, N. 7.(*i*)

*a*) Between mm. 84-85 and 88-9, C.V. has:

# Sonata in G Major, K521

C.V. Libro XIII, N.8. (i)

# Sonata in G Major, K522

C. V. Libro XIII, N. 9. *(i)*

# Sonata in G Major, K523

C. V. Libro XIII, N. 10. (e)

# Sonata in F Major, K524

C.V. Libro XIII, N. **11.** *(e)*

**7**_C.V.*a)*     **17**_ *b)* This measure is duplicated in C.V. **23**_C.V.*c)*

**24-26** (e **31-33,65-67,72-74**)_*d)* These passages consist of two mm. in all printed editions, but in C.V. the third measure is so clear and consistent that I felt it had to be included. **78**_C.V. *e)*

# Sonata in F Major, K525

C. V. Libro XIII, N. 12. (e)

28.-(e 29-31)_C. V.

**La correzione è fatta sul modello delle misure 69 e 71.**

*La correction est faite suivant le modèle des mesures 69 et 71.*

*La corrección está hecha inspirada en el modelo de los compases 69 y 71.*

The correction is made on the model of bars 69 and 71.

# Sonata in C Minor, K526

# Sonata in C Major, K527

C. V. Libro XIII, N. 14. *(t)*

# Sonata in B-flat Major, K528

# Sonata in B-flat Major, K529

# Sonata in E Major, K530

*Sonata in E Major, K530*    55

# Sonata in E Major, K531

C.V. Libro XIII, N. 18. *(e)*

# Sonata in A Minor, K532

(120)

(125)

(130)

(135)

(140)

(145)

(150)

(155)

C. V. Libro XIII, N. 19. *(e)*

# Sonata in A Major, K533

C. V. Libro XIII, N. 20. *(e)*

# Sonata in D Major, K534

C. V. Libro XIII, N. 21(i)

# Sonata in D Major, K535

**C.V. Libro XIII, N. 22.** *(e)*

# Sonata in A Major, K536

C.V. Libro XIII, N.**23.** *(i)*

**17 - C.V.** *a)*

# Sonata in A Major, K537

# Sonata in G Major, K538

# Sonata in G Major, K539

32-35 - a) Nel C. V. la nota bassa è *Si ♭*.
　　　　　 *Dans le C. V. la note basse est* Si ♭.

36-37 - b) Nel C. V. la nota bassa è *Sol*.
　　　　　 *Dans le C. V. la note basse est* Sol.

95-98 - c) Nel C. V. la nota bassa è *Mi ♭*.
　　　　　 *Dans le C. V. la note basse est* Mi ♭.

99-100 - d) Nel C. V. la nota bassa è *Do*.
　　　　　 *Dans le C. V. la note basse est* Do

*En el C. V. la nota baja es un* Si ♭.
In the C. V. the bass note is *B♭*.

*En el C. V. la nota baja es un* Sol.
In the C. V. the bass note is *G*.

*En el C. V. la nota baja es un* Mi ♭.
In the V. C. the bass note is *E♭*.

*En el C. V. la nota baja es un* Do.
In the C. V. the bass note is *C*.

# Sonata in F Major, K540

C.V. Libro XIII, N. 27. (i)

# Sonata in F Major, K541

C. V. Libro XIII, N. 28. (*i*)    (110)

21    (e simili)      (*y similes*)
      (*et semblubles*) - (and similar)

*a)*

# Sonata in F Major, K542

C. V. Libro XIII, N. 29.(i)

9 (e simili) | (y similes) | a)
(el semblables) | (and similar)

# Sonata in F Major, K543

104    *Sonata in F Major, K543*

# Sonata in B-flat Major, K544

C. S. Libro IV, N. 29. (e)

1 (e simili)        (y similes)        a) Formula del trillo:        Fórmula del trino:
  (et semblables)  (and similar)          Formule du trille:        Formula of the trill:

12 (e 31) - b) Nel testo, sotto le semicrome è scritto *Arbitrio*.        *En el texto, debajo de las semicorcheas kay escrito* Arbitrio.
          *Dans le texte, sous les doubles croches, on lit* Arbitrio.        In the text, under the semiquaver is written *Arbitrio*.

21 - C. S.   c)        40 - C. S.   d)

# Sonata in B-flat Major, K545

C. S. Libro IV, N. 30. *(e)*

32 - 34  (e 36-38) _ C. S.   *a)*

# Sonata in G Minor, K546

CODICE SANTINI, Libro IV, N. 31. *(i)*

*a)*

35 (e 46)   C. S.

# Sonata in G Major, K547

C. S. Libro IV, N. 32. *(i)*

66 - 72 - C. S.

# Sonata in C Major, K548

CODICE SANTINI, Libro IV, N.33.(i)

# Sonata in C Major, K549

CODICE SANTINI, Libro IV, N. 34. *(i)*

# Sonata in B-flat Major, K550

C. S. Libro IV, N. 35. *(t)*

# Sonata in B-flat Major, K551

C. S. Libro IV, N. 36. (e)

(95)

e simili - y similes
et semblables - and similar

C. S.

a) Dato l'andamento del pezzo e il procedimento del passo, sarebbe difficile e inopportuno un trillo di 7 note. È da preferirsi il mordente con questa esecuzione:

*Etant donné l'allure du morceau et la marche du passage, un trille de 7 notes serait difficile et inopportun. Le mordant est préférable exécuté comme suit:*

*Dada la estructura de la pieza y el procedimiento del pasaje, sería difícil y importuno un trino de 7 notas. Es preferible el mordiente con esta ejecución.*

Because of the movement of the piece and proceding of the passage, a trill of 7 notes will be difficult and inopportune. The mordent with this execution is preferred:

# Sonata in D Minor, K552

# Sonata in D Minor, K553

C. S. Libro IV, N. 38. (e)

146    *Sonata in D Minor, K553*

# Sonata in F Major, K554

*Sonata in F Major, K554*

C. S. Libro IV, N.39. (i)

# Sonata in F Minor, K555

CODICE SANTINI, Libro IV, N. 40. *(t)*